IMPROVE YOUR FLYCASTING

LOU STEVENS

SWAN·HILL
PRESS

First published in the UK in 1995
by Swan Hill Press
an imprint of Airlife Publishing Ltd

British Library Cataloguing in Publication Data
A catalogue record for this book
is available from the British Library

ISBN 1 85310 469 8

Printed in England by Livesey Ltd., Shrewsbury.

Swan Hill Press

an imprint of Airlife Publishing Ltd.
101 Longden Road, Shrewsbury SY3 9EB, England

IMPROVE YOUR FLYCASTING

Acknowledgements

With thanks to Eddie Bassin, my casting coach and mentor – the foundation he laid is still sound.

Contents

List of Figures

Preface

This book was written as a result of many conversations with anglers who were endeavouring to improve their casting skill. Also, from the experience gained during 'question and answer' periods at the Montreal School of Gamefishing.

It has been noted for years that the physical motions of casting are much better performed by those who fully understand why such motions are necessary.

Flycasting, although perhaps an art form, is not a natural talent, albeit some take longer to learn than others.

The desire to improve is the important factor, without the ability to be self-critical little progress is possible. It is of little use to read instructions from the comfort of a fireside chair, then try and put the theory into practice during a fishing day.

It is hoped that the principles outlined in the following pages will be practised (perhaps over grass in the local park — perhaps over the water of a nearby pond) well before they are put into use actually fishing.

If the desire is present any fly-fisher can become a competent caster with instruction and practice.

I wish all readers success with their endeavours.

Lou Stevens
Alvaston
Derbyshire

Chapter 1

How Can We Improve?

It is the opinion of most casting instructors that good flycasting cannot be learned from the written word alone. Very few people, never having handled a fly-rod before, are capable of following written instructions to the point of casting proficiency. However, this does not mean that under the right circumstances the written word cannot be extremely useful.

Very few fly-fishermen attend professional casting schools, most take up the sport under the watchful eye of a fishing friend. It may well appear to the novice that the friend performs miraculous feats with his casting and will be the perfect instructor. Sadly, this is seldom so and a visit to a professional instructor would soon illustrate this point. The friend, who probably learned from a friend, passes on a number of bad habits that have been honed to a fine point. The novice, unable to separate the good from the bad, practises the bad habits until he too, in turn, has perfected them.

The result of this sequence of events can be seen at any waterside. Struggling anglers — albeit catching some fish — are fishing way below their potential, often without knowing why. Sometimes tackle is blamed and a new rod or line is purchased in the belief that it will improve matters. Trade advertising is largely responsible for this state of affairs and is often intentionally directed towards the novice in difficulties.

Of course a good rod, and a good line, can help in the casting process, but some of the claims made for various products and materials are bordering on the ludicrous. First must come knowledge of the correct procedure, only then can the aspiring angler make full use of the potential that is on offer. Even more important, having acquired a degree of skill the angler will be in a much better position to know exactly what will help and what will hinder further progress.

Without doubt a good casting school is a short cut to success, but the fact must be faced that so very few anglers avail themselves of this facility. One of the main reasons for this approach is the catching of fish, particularly from small private stillwaters. Often such fish can be taken with the minimum of casting ability, consequently success in the bag does away with the urgency of casting instruction. It is believed that progress has been made, and will continue to be made with further experience. A visit to the river to fish for wild browns would be shock treatment indeed and quickly destroy the illusion.

Quite a number of fly-fishermen fully appreciate their lack of casting ability and try very hard to achieve improvement, often promising themselves professional help sometime in the future. When it comes to the choice of a day's fishing or a day's instruction, the fishing wins and the thought of instruction remains just that. It is a curious fact that trying to overcome difficulties, or improve prowess without an instructor, will often cause a number of secondary problems to develop that will worsen things rather than make an improvement.

It is at this point that the written word becomes useful. Most certainly, well written instruction will enable the discerning angler to recognise many built-in faults. Most certainly, practise to eliminate such faults will bring marked improvement. So, the widely held belief that casting cannot be learned from a book is only partially true. Improved casting can most certainly be learned from the written word by those who are prepared to be self critical of their performance.

In the following pages it is intended to cover casting as it applies to trout, and salmon casting has been left out. The techniques of casting for stillwater rainbows, wild river browns, and to a large extent sea-trout, are somewhat similar. Salmon technique, using salmon equipment, is a large enough subject to require separate treatment elsewhere. However, it should be borne in mind that an efficient approach to trout fishing is a good foundation for future salmon fishing — the knowledge will not be wasted.

Good casting is a joy to watch and is considered by many to be a sport in itself. It is truly an art form that can be learned, and intense pleasure obtained when the result lives up to the expectation. The thrill of catching fish is an added bonus.

It is all very well maintaining that casting efficiency can be obtained by studying the written word and eliminating bad habits and faulty techniques, but a further factor must also be taken into consideration. Only by determination will the angler succeed in becoming a good caster. Bad habits and technique practised for years are hard to eradicate permanently. It is only too easy to make adjustments, be quite thrilled with the better results, then to slowly revert to the old ways under the pressure of catching fish. A whole new approach has to become second nature, and for a considerable period each cast will have to be mentally analysed. Work on it, the results will make it worthwhile. Sooner or later it will become an automatic process, and the full joy of fly-fishing will be there for the taking. Nothing of value in this world is obtained without some effort and the proficient casting of a fly is no exception.

Chapter 2

The Principle Involved

Fly-rods have several functions quite apart from casting, and these aspects of rod design will be fully dealt with a little later. At this stage it is essential to concentrate solely on the rod's function in the casting procedure, and to ignore everything else.

If we think of the rod as nothing more than a length of springy material, with a handle to grip at one end, we will focus our thoughts correctly. It has often been said that casting is a similar process to that performed by small boys in an unruly classroom who flick pellets from the tip of a ruler. The ruler is held upright at the base while a soggy wad of blotting paper is mounted on the tip, the tip is then drawn back and released to project the soggy wad. Yes, the ruler is being used as a spring to project the missile, but tension in the ruler is physically set up by pulling the tip back, not exactly the way we cast a fly!

However, this avenue of thought is in the right direction. We hold the rod (the spring), steady at the base while the rod tip is pulled back. In our case it is the line that activates the 'spring', aided by our manipulation of the base (the rod handle). We must fully appreciate that the line is an elongated streamlined weight, nothing more, and it is the line that is projected towards the target. Leader and fly just 'go along for the ride'.

Although a fly-line may not appear to be a heavy item, it is extremely so when compared to the area of its cross-section. When multiplied by its speed through the air (between 50mph and 70mph at the line tip), the force generated is considerable.

The technique of bringing the spring (the rod) into play by activating the weight (the line) at the rod tip, is what flycasting is all about.

The word 'technique' was deliberately used above to make it

16

absolutely clear that very little muscular strength is required — purely 'technique'. Any attempt to make a cast by brute force is doomed to failure.

The technique of casting is based on timing, so that line acceleration can be obtained to increase the force exerted at the rod tip. Once all thought of muscle power is put aside the technique of handling the rod to achieve the timing required comes quite easily.

Of course, the manual actions need to be correctly controlled. However, these points will be covered fully when we discuss various casts, here we must concentrate on the principle involved so that we fully understand exactly what we are trying to achieve.

Invariably a fly-rod is clearly marked with the recommended line weight. Often a range of weights is given, *i.e.* 4/5 or 5/6/7. Line manufacturers comply with the Association of Fishing Tackle Manufacturers' guide-lines, and all lines are specified by AFTM numbers that refer to weight. Each number represents a specific weight of 30ft of line excluding the level line tip. Various manufacturers produce lines differing considerably in diameter, but the weight will be consistent with the stated AFTM number. Diameter will also vary between lines designed to sink and those designed to float.

Generally speaking, a smaller diameter line of the correct AFTM number will out-perform its fatter counterpart, mainly because of reduced wind resistance.

The rating on a rod is based on 30ft of line beyond the rod tip, *i.e.* a rod rated No.5 will produce its full potential as a 'spring' when 30ft of AFTM No.5 line is in the air beyond the rod tip. Or will it? Not quite, as we shall see.

We have already considered the fact that acceleration times line weight represents the force exerted at the rod tip, consequently it automatically follows that a line of a specific AFTM number cannot be relied on to always produce a stated force. It all depends on the acceleration. Obviously a caster who is able to generate a greater acceleration than normally produced exerts a greater force at the rod tip, perhaps equal to a heavier weight line. The reverse is also true.

It therefore pays to accept the given rod rating purely as an indication of suitable line weight, then to try several lines of varying weights before a final decision is made.

Consideration must also be given to the length of fly-line that is habitually extended beyond the rod tip. As a very approximate rule of thumb 6ft of line represents a single rating against the AFTM scale, *i.e.* 36ft of AFTM No.5 line would approximate 30ft of AFTM No.6 line.

So, apart from the average acceleration produced, the average length of line aerialised during the casting must also be taken into account. This is another reason for trying a variety of lines whilst performing one's own particular brand of casting.

Normally it is only necessary to try lines one up or one down from the rod rating — and fishing friends or the tackle dealer will often oblige — but it does make a marked difference to results.

Now what about rods with multiple ratings? It is often advocated by tackle dealers that a rod with a double rating, *i.e.* 6/7, is so marked because the lower number refers to a double taper line (specified as AFTM 6 DT) while the higher number refers to a weight forward line (specified as AFTM 7 WF). When rods have a third rating, *i.e.* 6/7/8, it is said that the No.8 refers to the shooting head.

A very plausible theory, and like all plausible theories it has an element of fact. Yes, under certain conditions it may well be that a longer length of double taper line will be beyond the rod tip than is usual with a weight forward line, but conditions are rarely that consistent. A shooting head may be made up of any weight line — depending entirely on its length — and we will discuss the make-up of these heads a little later.

A good approach to a rod with multiple ratings is to take the middle number, then to test various lines as recommended previously using a full double taper or weight forward version depending on your choice.

A word of warning: always use a floating line for test purposes, even if the tests are carried out in the local park over grass. A line manufactured to sink is normally much thinner than one manufactured to float, and the lower wind resistance may give a totally false impression of the acceleration normally produced.

When testing a line for correct weight the caster needs to pay particular attention to the precise moment when the back-cast is fully extended. The procedure should be to measure out 30ft of line beyond the rod tip before casting commences, then using this 30ft length a few gentle casts are made to get the feel of the line. If the line feels right, normal casting is commenced. As mentioned above, the final decision is made when assessing the back-cast. At the precise moment the back-cast is fully extended a slight tug should be felt on the rod tip, 'slight' is the operative word. Provided a line maintains its height in the air during the casting process, *and* exerts a 'slight' tug on the rod tip during the back-cast, we have balanced line to rod.

All the above explanations really add up to the fact that to obtain optimum 'spring tension' from the rod, a line must be selected by the personal testing of the individual caster. A manufacturer's rating should be looked upon purely as a guide.

Any fly-fisherman who ignores this fact and slavishly adheres to the given rating may well place himself under a permanent handicap to improvement.

Let us now consider the tackle we will use to make our casts.

Chapter 3

The Tackle We Use

It is not intended that the following will be a general discourse on tackle, nor is it intended to advocate any specific item of tackle, such discussions are not the concern of these pages. Various items of tackle will be discussed but purely in the light of how they affect casting. At the same time it is necessary to have a good insight into what is available, and to understand thoroughly the potential of the tackle we use. All good workmen understand the function of their tools, only a bad workman blames the tools for the results of his work.

The Rod

Over the past few years rod manufacture and design has changed radically. Not so very long ago a rod of split-cane was considered the ultimate casting implement and many still hold that view, but today the majority of rods in use contain carbon fibre.

During the heyday of split-cane there were many examples of poor quality rods on the market, and exactly the same applies to rods of carbon fibre. Unfortunately for the angler there are no recognised standards of manufacture or of carbon fibre content. Many so-called carbon rods offered for sale are little better than glass fibre with a minimum unspecified carbon content. Trade names only add to the confusion with such descriptions as 'cross-weave', 'diamond-weave', 'continuous fibre' etc. Rods are also available in 'Kevlar' and 'Boron', plus a variety of materials expressed as numbers or letters.

So what constitutes a good rod that will not impair all our efforts? Not an easy question to answer.

The old saying, 'you get what you pay for', probably holds good provided the rod comes from a quality manufacturer. The difficulty — these days — is to know which manufacturers come into that category. Advertising is such a powerful weapon that many tackle companies have become a 'household name' by use of the media. Their products do not always live up to the advertising. This is particularly applicable to some of the companies with mass manufacturing in the Far East. When purchasing a new rod a lot of discretion has to be used. Nevertheless, do not expect to purchase a good rod, correctly designed, at a price that should tell you that this is impossible.

Quite apart from the design and quality, rods come in a variety of lengths, weights and line ratings. For our discussion it is only necessary to consider rods that vary in length between 7ft and 11ft. Certainly rods are readily available outside those limits, but they require variation in the basic casting techniques to realise their full potential. Also, rods between 7ft and 11ft are quite capable of covering all trout fishing needs.

The weight of a rod is important to good casting, and a good quality carbon rod should have a weight very similar to the scale shown below.

Rod Length	Line Rating	Average Weight
7ft	4	2¼ — 2¾oz
7ft 6in	5	2½ — 3oz
8ft 6in	6	3 — 3¼oz
9ft	6	3 — 3½oz
9ft 6in	6	3¼ — 3¾oz
10ft	7	3½ — 4oz
11ft	8	3½ — 4¼oz

Excessive weight usually results in a top-heavy rod, making line acceleration most difficult to achieve without the wrist becoming very tired. Any single-handed rod over 6oz in weight will require a special casting technique to overcome this problem.

The length chosen rather depends on the type of fishing usually carried out. Very generally speaking all rods between 7ft and 10ft are quite capable of making similar length casts, their design compensating for the varying length. A long rod will not necessarily increase your distance of casting, only your casting prowess will bring distance results. Nor will a longer heavier rod, rated for a heavier line, necessarily achieve distance. No, a particular rod length and line rating should be chosen to suit the fishing needs. Short rods are more useful on small streams where overhanging foliage is often a problem; longer rods allow higher back-casts to overcome tall bankside

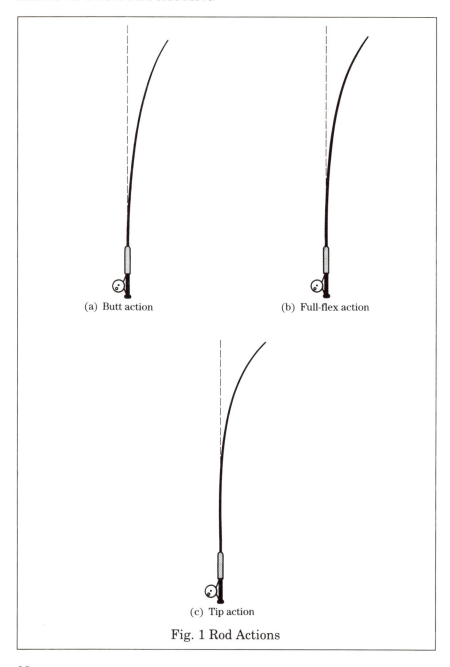

(a) Butt action   (b) Full-flex action

(c) Tip action

Fig. 1 Rod Actions

vegetation. Match the rod and line weight to your fishing needs, achieve distance with technique.

The 'action' of a rod may be described as tip-action, full-flex action, or butt-action. (See Fig. 1) Past theories on the merits of the various actions were convenient but not always sound. Tip-action rods were often described as having a 'dry fly action', whilst those with butt action were called 'wet fly rods'. The French even describe full-flex rods as 'parabolic' and 'long-cast' models.

The truth of the matter is simply that tip-action rods are able to generate their spring power with a minimum of line in the air, and consequently cast a tight loop of line. This is a useful action on small streams, particularly where considerable accuracy is required. Rods with full-flex action are really general purpose rods, having the ability to generate considerable line acceleration for distance, hold a tight loop, and at the same time maintain accuracy. Butt-action rods are rarely found among carbon rods, it is really a glass fibre or split-cane action. Such a rod can be quite useful if heavy flies or lures are regularly used. The line acceleration is slow, resulting in a wide loop, and distance will be something of a problem.

Again, select the action of a rod to suit your fishing needs.

When making a purchase attention should be given to the rod fittings. A reel seat that allows an 'up mounting' of the reel (just below the cork handle) is an advantage when casting. The weight of the reel is closer to the wrist and less likely to cause wrist bend or fatigue. Rod rings are the subject of much advertising 'hype', and some of the new-style 'super rings' are not all that robust. Old style hard chrome snake rings are hard to beat, they wear well, are easy to replace, and cause little line friction. A very important point is the ring spacing on the rod, especially at the tip end. For good casting make very sure that the first rod ring is no more than 6in from the rod tip. If this is not so, then time spent altering the position will pay handsome dividends. When the rod flexes under fast line acceleration the bend at the rod tip is considerable, the first rod ring in the wrong position will cause excessive friction. (See Fig. 2)

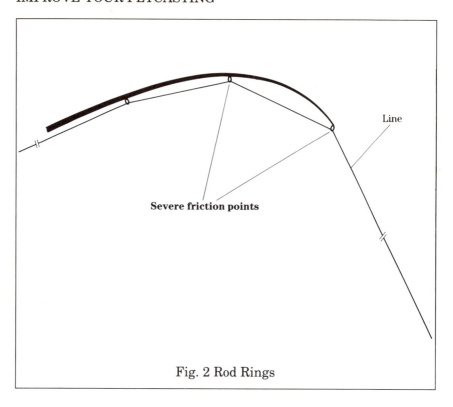

Line

Severe friction points

Fig. 2 Rod Rings

Reels

Reels have almost no function in the casting process. Various designs of reels, and the quality of manufacture, have considerable bearing on practical fishing, but during casting — which could easily be performed without a reel — they have little importance.

Reels only enter the equation when they are of a type to influence the rod action. It used to be said that reels should be carefully selected to balance the rod. What a lot of nonsense! A reel should be unobtrusive, it should never be used to counteract a top-heavy rod, the result is simply disastrous to the casting process. Little wonder that champion casters do away with reels entirely during casting tournaments.

To be unobtrusive a reel needs to be in the normal range of single action reels compatible with the line size. The following list will illustrate this point.

Average Size	Average Weight	Line Size
3in dia	4oz	5 + backing
3¼in dia	4¼oz	6 + backing
3½in dia	4½oz	7 + backing
3¾in dia	6oz	8 + backing

Although double action, (geared ratio retrieve), and automatic reels, are sometimes attractive for their ability to control line during actual fishing, their excessive weights do nothing to help casting performance.

By all means select a reel design that suits your fishing needs, but be mindful to keep within the above guide-lines if you wish your casting to improve without hindrance.

Lines

Mostly due to the needs of the stillwater angler a large variety of line types is now on offer. Floating lines, intermediate lines, sink-tip lines, slow sinking, fast sinking, and 'depth-charge' (!) Most are available in double taper, weight forward, and shooting head.

Double taper floating, intermediate, and slow/fast sinking lines raise no special problems during casting. In fact, the intermediate and sinking lines somewhat aid casting by their smaller diameter generating less wind resistance. Sink-tip lines are always difficult to cast because their density changes along their length. The 'depth-charge' or 'lead-head' types are usually restricted to shooting heads.

Provided none of the thin running-line of a weight forward line is outside the rod tip during casting, no major difference will be experienced between weight forward and double taper lines. A weight forward line may well result in the capability of longer casts, but certainly casting accuracy and finesse will be sacrificed. The accuracy and finesse obtained using shooting heads is also quite poor.

It was mentioned earlier that shooting heads could be of any weight line. If the earlier comments on various lengths of line equalling different weights was clearly followed, then the following procedure to select a shooting head will also be clear.

Let us suppose that a rod is rated for a No.6 line. A length of, say, a No.7 line could be fed out beyond the rod tip during a normal casting action, when it felt comfortable and correct it could be carefully measured. It may well be that the length of No.7 line measures only 22ft to 24ft. No matter, that length plus 18in constitutes a shooting head for the rod. In this way any weight line can be used, and the length of shooting head will vary accordingly.

Leaders

Any discourse on leaders is made extremely difficult by the exaggerated claims made in the angling press. Claims of leaders over 24ft being used as standard practice lead others to believe that they should be able to follow suit. Claims have even been made that level leaders over 20ft in length are commonly used.

It is hard to understand why such claims are made, surely no angler of any substance needs to enhance his reputation in such a manner.

Common sense will tell us that a leader, over half the length of all aerialised line, cannot turn over in a nicely formed loop during the cast.

Very few anglers, even accomplished casters, are capable of smoothly casting a leader that is longer than 15ft. A leader of 12ft would give even better results. Research carried out by Dr G. Byrnes, a resident ophthalmologist in the USA, has shown that the visual acuity of trout is some fourteen times less than humans. Although a trout can see sudden movement at quite a distance, everything beyond a few feet is somewhat blurred. Of course we want to keep our fly-line well away from the wary trout — but over 24ft is rather ridiculous!

The most important point about any leader is the ability to land on the water with finesse, and at the same time not to impair casting.

To carry out this function the leader must be tapered, have a heavy butt section to aid transference of energy from the line, and have a tippet thickness in keeping with the size of the fly being used.

The new braided leaders usually have a heavy butt section and accept transfer of energy easily. If a 5ft braided leader is used, to which is attached a 7½ft of tapered nylon, a nicely balanced 12½ft leader is the result.

Think about your tackle; good, well balanced tackle will not, necessarily, enable you to cast any better, but at least it will not hold back your progress.

Chapter 4

Fundamentals

At this stage the reader may well be wondering when we are going to commence casting.

The fact is that we have been building our casting from the opening pages. A house cannot be built without a foundation if the final result is to be sound, so far we have been laying down a solid foundation on which we can build.

The comment from many anglers that they thoroughly understand the theory of casting, but just cannot put it into practice, is a sure sign of a faulty foundation. Not only must we understand casting principles, and the function of our tackle, we must also understand certain fundamentals. The combination of principles, tackle usage, and fundamental procedure, add up to the sound foundation we are seeking.

The Grip on the Rod
The first consideration is that 'grip' is a poor description of what we are trying to achieve. We are really discussing how we 'hold' the rod and 'what' we hold.

Handles of rods should be of good quality smooth cork, as this material has a cushioning effect that is non-slip and allows a firm hold without a vice-like grip. Handles of composition material, or those of synthetic cork, do not have the same faculty. Nearly all rod handles are mass produced with standard diameters, but sometimes this creates a difficulty. Extra large, or extremely small hands, might have a problem with standard handles, and consequently casting is affected. If you are faced with this difficulty (and only a few are) then steps need to be taken to remedy the situation.

Rod handles also come in a variety of shapes, such as scroll, cigar, full-wells, half-wells, western, super fine or midge. In most cases the

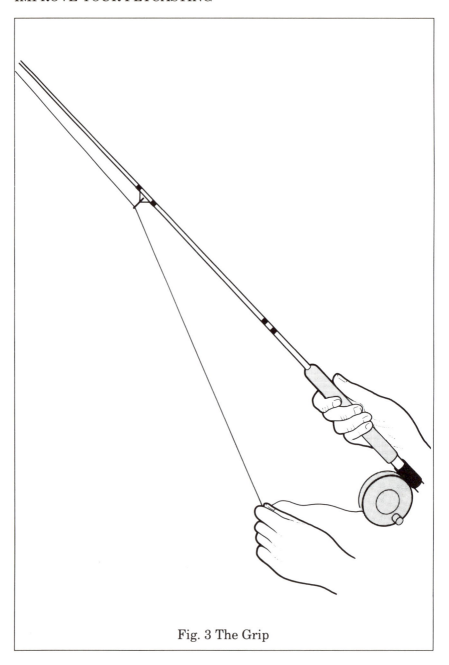

Fig. 3 The Grip

shape has been a very careful decision by the makers of the rod, and the design suits the rod ideally and will not influence casting.

We do not 'grip' a rod handle, we hold it firmly in one of three ways.
1 With the thumb on top parallel with the rod
2 With the thumb to the side
3 At times with the forefinger extended on top instead of the thumb.
Most casters employ the first hold. (*See* Fig.3)

The cork handle should be long enough for the holding hand, with the hand more towards the top of the handle than the bottom. It should not be necessary, if your outfit is well balanced, to move the position of the hand to overcome a top-heavy feeling.

Rod Angle

The rod, when held perpendicular, should be absolutely vertical with the reel facing towards the front. At no time must the rod be allowed to lean to a side angle during casting. All rod movement, both forward and back, must be in the same vertical plane. This point cannot be over-emphasised — it is the most common casting fault.

A rod that lays over to the side, usually to the right with a right-handed caster, cannot fail to lose at least twenty per cent of line acceleration. If the reel points outwards as well, then even more line acceleration is lost.

The only exceptions to the above rule are when deliberate side-casts are made, and at a certain point in the roll-cast. However, more on that later.

Coupled with the fault of laying the rod out to the side is the fault of the extended arm. With the length of spring available to us (the length of the rod), it is extremely difficult to understand why some anglers feel they need additional leverage. During the forward and backwards cast there is no need whatever to wave the casting arm about, the elbow should hang loosely to the side. The forearm alone will generate the rod movement we need. If we remember this, and keep the rod always in the same vertical plane, many of our casting difficulties will disappear.

It is highly probable that the main reason for laying a rod out to the side could be the view of the line during casting. Our eyes play tricks as we commence the back-cast, it appears that the line is being propelled straight back towards us. It is an optical illusion. The line is, in fact, being propelled upwards as well as back, and will pass over our heads at a greater height than the length of the rod. Have faith! (*See* Fig.4)

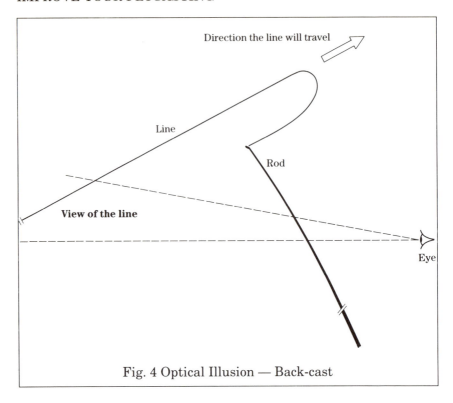

Fig. 4 Optical Illusion — Back-cast

Remember the basic principle: we need to generate line acceleration so that the acceleration times line weight will exert force on our spring, (the rod). The loss of twenty to twenty-five per cent of the acceleration due to faulty rod angle must rate as a very major fault.

Stance
It has been noted for years that the majority of anglers create difficulties for themselves by paying scant attention to their stance during casting. It would seem only natural for a right-handed caster to place his left foot forward, and left-handed casters vice versa. It is wrong! It is one of the reasons for not keeping the rod in a vertical plane during the cast. Try this out for yourself, indoors with the butt only, and it will quickly become apparent how easily the upper arm extends away from the body and the rod lays over when the wrong foot is placed forward.

A simple thing, like placing the correct foot forward, immediately improves casting technique.

Of course, the correct foot is easy to remember when casting from the bank whilst standing, but not so easy to do when kneeling to cast, or when wading. The point of placing the correct foot forward is so that the body is quarter-angled against the cast. Right-handed casters right foot forward, body quarter-angled to the left; left-handed casters vice versa. There is no difficulty maintaining this body angle whilst kneeling or wading.

Line Handling

Little needs to be said here except that all casting should be performed with the line held by the non-casting hand. A firm grip of the line between the butt ring and the reel is essential. It is a mistake to attempt to cast while the line is direct to the reel, or the line is held trapped by the casting hand. (*See* Fig.3)

It is quite common to see stillwater anglers stripping off yards of line from the reel prior to casting. The stripped line is usually left to lie on the ground. This is a very bad habit that impairs casting efficiency and endangers the line. During casting the line will invariably catch in some bank-side vegetation and snag the cast; even worse, the line is often trodden on and damaged.

During initial casting, and the extending of line, it is better for line to be drawn from the reel by the line-holding hand. The line being drawn off and fed into the forward-cast as required. When retrieving to cast again, the line should be held in loose loops by the line-hand, then each loop can be fed out into the next cast in the same manner as line was stripped from the reel.

A lot more trouble? Maybe, but casting will be improved and expensive lines will last very much longer.

Wrist Action

It is at this point that we enter the field of controversy. Practically all casting instructors have their own individual view of the function of the wrist during casting. Some advocate casting from the wrist, others advise the caster to keep a relaxed wrist, then there are those who maintain that the wrist should be kept firm. A most confusing picture; the student of casting may well feel that progress is almost impossible when the instructors cannot agree.

In truth there is something to be said for all these theories, no-one is actually wrong, for the situation is a little more subtle than at first appears. Certainly good casts can be made from the wrist by a very skilled caster, and a relaxed wrist correctly performing its function is close to the ideal, but we have not yet reached that standard. An angler wishing to improve his casting has to learn to overcome built-in faults before a high degree of skill can be attained.

So, it is necessary to over-emphasize what is required, and to build up good habits, then, and only then, will the relaxed approach become second nature.

For our purpose we must insist that the wrist should stay firm; a break of the wrist at this stage of progress would result in the rod being carried too far back during the back-cast. If a rod being out of the vertical plane (laying to the side) is a major fault, then the rod being carried back beyond the perpendicular is in the same category.

It is most difficult, almost impossible, to stop a rod in the 12 o'clock position if the wrist is slack, or breaks at the end of the back-cast. A skilled caster can handle this difficulty, an improver cannot cope at all.

The correct action of the wrist during casting can be practised in the garden, and such practise will soon illustrate exactly what is required. Take a hammer out of the tool box and visit the garden fence, then spend a while hammering imaginary nails into an upright fence post. Carefully analyse each stroke of the hammer, note the action of the wrist — relaxed, but held firm — note that the forearm delivers the stroke, not the upper arm. Note that the elbow is naturally close to the side. Hammer in a few more imaginary nails until the action is firmly established in the mind — now you are using the wrist correctly!

When actually casting with a rod, it may, at first, be difficult to maintain the correct wrist action. The old trick of tucking the end of the rod into the shirt cuff could help. Another way is to carry a 12in strip of Velcro fastener in your pocket, fastening the strip round the reel seat and wrist. Whatever way you tackle this problem it will only be temporary until the 'feel' becomes natural.

Chapter 5

Basic Casting

'No man is born an artist
so no man is born an angler'

(Izaak Walton,
The Compleat Angler 1653)

No angler should ever reach the stage where he believes he fully understands the theory of flycasting, but has decided further improvement is impossible. We can all improve no matter how well we cast, perfection is a target not an accomplishment.

Enough has been said about the principles involved, and the basic fundamentals, at this stage we should be fully prepared to see how it all comes together when we commence casting.

Although mindful that there are a number of different casts which will have to be persevered with in due course, for the moment we shall concentrate on the basic casting technique. Again that word 'technique', for it is the key to all progress.

It will be noted that all advice is given for right-handed casters; left-handers will be used to the process of reversing the information.

The Mental Picture

By developing a mental picture of what we are trying to achieve, we will attain an 'actual' result close to our requirement.

First draw line off the reel so that a measured 30ft of line is beyond the rod tip. Then draw off an additional 3ft — 4ft so that there is spare line to be held in the left hand. If the practice session is over grass, which is recommended at this stage, lay out the line straight in front of the rod.

Take hold of the rod in your right hand without trapping the line, holding the line coming from the butt ring in the fingers of the left

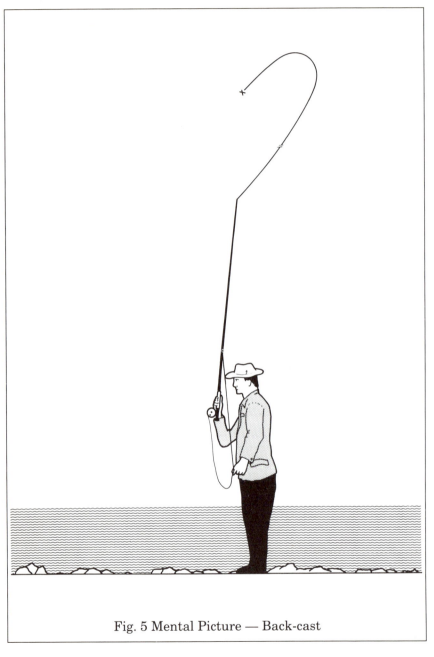

Fig. 5 Mental Picture — Back-cast

hand. (*See* Fig.3) Make sure your stance is correct, right elbow hanging loosely at your side, the rod pointing straight ahead down the line. Right, we are ready to commence a back-cast.

The mental picture of what we are about to perform should be that we intend to project the line up to the clouds above our heads. Not backwards, but upwards high above our heads. So, we start to raise the rod, slowly at first to take up all the slack, then we accelerate the movement until the rod is at the perpendicular. Now we stop, not allowing any further backward movement of the rod. At this point the rod handle should be below your right cheek. (*See* Fig.5)

Points to remember:

1 Correct hold of rod/line and stance

2 Rod in correct vertical plane — not leaning out to the side

3 Wrist held firmly, upper arm and elbow hanging down loosely

4 A smooth acceleration to the perpendicular
   — no force, no jerky movements

5 Line projected up towards the clouds

At the completion of the back-cast, when the rod is perpendicular, we should have a mental picture of the line extending out towards the clouds. Fine, so give a slight pause while you imagine the line unfurling. Just when your mental picture tells you that the line has almost straightened out — a very slight tug at the rod tip — you can commence the forward-cast.

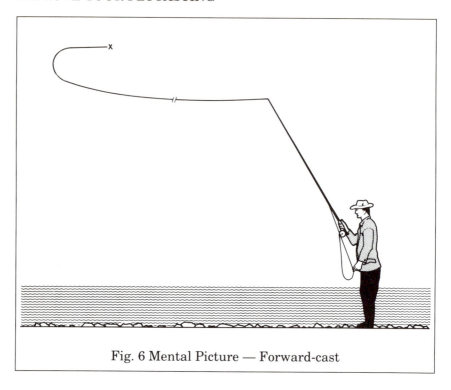

Fig. 6 Mental Picture — Forward-cast

The rod is now brought forward, not with as much acceleration that you put into the back-cast, but with a good sharp tap, reminiscent of how you practised hammering those imaginary nails into the fence post. The mental picture is to project the line straight forward above eye level. (*See* Fig.6)

Points to remember:

1 Keep the rod in the same vertical plane

2 Keep the wrist firm — upper arm and elbow hanging down loosely

3 A 'hammer-tap' forward
   — not the fast acceleration as in the back-cast

4 Project the line out above eye level — don't lower your rod too far

Actual Picture

You have now completed a back-cast and forward-cast. We will stop at this point to analyse the results.

If you have carried out the motions correctly the line will have been projected straight out behind you on the back-cast, nice and high. (*See* Fig.7) When the back-cast was complete the line would have loaded the rod as a 'spring' ready to project the line forward. With your 'hammer-tap' forward the 'spring' would have been brought into play and the forward-cast commenced. Your attempt to project the line forward above eye level resulted in an almost level forward-cast. (*See* Fig.8)

After some practice of the above technique, difficulties may, nevertheless, still be with us. The answer must be to go back to basic fundamentals — you cannot build a sound house on a shaky foundation. The stance, the vertical plane of the rod, the wrist action, the stopping of the rod in a perpendicular position, plus a smooth non-jerky acceleration into the back-cast — all will influence the results obtained.

We have left out of the above equation the question of timing, and deliberately so. It has already been mentioned that casting technique is really based on timing, but first we must get our basics correct so that we are able to apply timing to them.

Anyone who has seen service in the armed forces will remember the old drill timing of 1—2-3—1, (one — two three — one), the 2-3 being the pause between two drill movements. Casting is almost an identical situation, *i.e.* back-cast (1), pause (2-3), forward-cast (1). If necessary count out loud as you perform the actions.

Of course, we must bear in mind that the longer the line cast the longer must be the pause to allow the line to straighten out — but this is a matter of instinct, plus feeling that slight tug at the rod-tip.

Fig. 7 Actual Back-cast

Fig. 8 Actual Forward-cast

Continuing Our Progress

So far we have completed a false cast in the air. The forward-cast may be accelerated into the back-cast once again, or, it may be terminated so as to deliver the line to the water.

There are several reasons the false casting may be continued:

1 In dry fly fishing to dry the fly
2 to judge distance and direction
3 to feed out more line.

The first two reasons are self-explanatory but feeding out the line needs an explanation.

Feeding Line (Shooting Line)

It is quite in order to shoot a little line into the forward-cast during false casting in order to lengthen the cast. This is always done on the forward-cast, never the back-cast.

Whilst accelerating into the back-cast, the left hand holding the line is extended out to the left to draw line from the reel. As the forward-cast unfurls to the front, the drawn off line is allowed to slide through the fingers of the left hand — into the forward-cast. At no time must the left hand lose contact and control of the line. Before commencing a new back-cast the left hand must, once again, grip the line very firmly. The timing of this procedure is quite easy and it quickly becomes a natural action.

The above procedure can also be used at the end of the cast, before the line settles on the water. The result will be that the fly alights gently, there will be no tendency to bounce back due to the forward motion of the line ending abruptly.

We must now deal with the situation where the forward-cast is terminated so as to place the fly on the water. It calls for a variation in the final forward-cast.

All is the same until the line is unfurling in front of us at slightly below eye level. At this point the rod arm is extended so that the rod is in line with the falling line. The rod now follows the line down to the water — it FOLLOWS the line, it does NOT PRECEDE it.

Correctly carried out, this movement results in the rod pointing at the fly as it arrives on the water surface. It has been described as poking your thumb in the fish's eye — not a bad description.

Retrospect

We now have a back-cast, followed by a forward-cast, correctly made with 30ft of line. The final result is a cast of 30ft of line, plus 3ft of line from the final shoot, plus 9ft rod length, plus 12ft leader length, plus 3ft arm length. A total cast of 57ft. Nothing to complain about!

Chapter 6

More Distance?

We have all read articles in the angling press that claim a full fly-line (30yd) had been cast without difficulty. Never having seen such a feat performed by any angler whilst fishing it is hard to make comment. Mostly, claims of this nature are made when certain brands of tackle are being discussed or reviewed. Let us be very clear on this, no item of tackle is going to become a magic wand that will transform your casting overnight. Good tackle is always a help — but it is never the complete answer.

We have already seen that a normal back and forward-cast with only 30ft of line in use, will result in a final cast of some 57ft. How much further distance do you need? Let us ponder the question.

If you are a river fisherman the probable answer is that casts in excess of 57ft are only rarely required. The stillwater angler might have a different point of view. Small private stillwaters are usually no problem, but reservoirs are a very different matter.

When confronted with the huge expanse of water of a reservoir the average angler is often overwhelmed — the fish could be anywhere, and are probably out of reach of our casting. Our casting length seems so puny in relation to the expanse of water. Then there are those rises, so clearly visible and tempting, yet well outside our casting range. Another problem is that thoughtless fellow angler who has waded out some 5 to 10yd and disturbed the water — surely all fish are now somewhere out in the centre. Distance casting must be the answer!

No, not always. Without going into various fishing skills the answer may be much simpler. Why not keep away from thoughtless wading anglers? Why not try and remember that undisturbed fish very often feed in the margins? Try to remember that nearly all the fish you have ever caught have been within 10yd of the bank — regardless of the original cast.

Of course it is very desirable to be able to execute a longer cast when needed, but try not to fall into the trap of continual long casting. Every day at the waterside you will see anglers struggling to put out longer and longer casts — it's a funny thing, they are not necessarily the ones who are catching the fish! Long casts very rarely land on the water with finesse, they are likely to disturb more fish than they catch.

The skilled caster places his fly with accuracy and finesse, right in the zone where the fish are feeding, and at the same time has the ability to make a longer cast when it is needed.

Before we consider the technique of long casting, let us remember that line acceleration times line-weight exerts the force to activate the spring in our rod. We cannot alter the rod or the line weight, so very obviously we must increase the line acceleration. We know that brute force cannot do the job for us so we need a technique.

Single and Double-Haul Casting
Most fly-fishermen have heard of 'hauling', some practise the technique, sadly so very few do it properly. Often results are very poor, even 'double-hauling' barely increases the casting distance.

You will often see anglers with their line-holding hand flashing up and down alarmingly — one moment on their hip, then up to their head, then down again. The cast, when completed, is little more than 60ft. The truth of the matter is that a 'haul' on the line by the line hand **is only effective during the power movement of the rod**. *i.e.* at the precise moment you sweep the rod upwards into the back-cast, and at the precise moment you tap forward (hammer-like) into the forward-cast. At all other times the 'haul' is wasted.

Another important fact, a 'haul' is only intended to put more bend into the rod to increase the force on the line. **Any haul of more than a few inches is a waste of time**.

Watch a really good caster double-hauling; the hauling action is short and concise, just a hard tug on the line at exactly the right moment. Line acceleration is increased to the point that he can 'shoot' yards of line into the final forward-cast.

The 'single-haul' is mainly used when performing the motions of a back-cast, rarely on the forward-cast. Nearly all good casters use this technique every time they cast, as on its own the single-haul enables several yards of line to 'shoot' into the forward-cast. The result can be a cast of approximately 63 to 72ft.

The double-haul will add much more — how much more depends on your technique — and very long casts are commonly obtained.

It must always be appreciated that a double-haul does nothing to enhance the accuracy or finesse of a cast. It is the haul on the forward-cast that does the damage. A single-haul on the back-cast will enable the forward-cast to be made under much better control.

A good caster will make a normal cast for distances of up to 60ft, then will single-haul to reach out a little further. Double-hauling will be reserved for those special situations when distance is the criteria — and finesse is not so important.

Distance into the Wind

Wind is the enemy of the fly-fisher, and many anglers overcome the problem by running away from it. Have a look around any stillwater when there is a good wind blowing, you will see that a very large percentage of anglers have moved position so that they do not have to cast into the wind.

We all know — or should know — that the trout food, nymphs etc., gather on the downwind shore, and that is where the fish will be provided the water is warm enough. Consequently, to fish correctly it is often very necessary to cast into an onshore wind.

The single or double-haul will help to some extent, but in a strong wind the forward-cast will always give difficulty.

The way to overcome the problem is to 'side-cast'.

The Side-cast

The side-cast takes advantage of the fact that the wind is not nearly so intense just above the water surface. A good side-cast will keep the forward-cast at a height less than 3ft above the water.

First things first. Before attempting a side-cast reverse your stance, right-handers place the left foot forward and angle the body to the right, left-handers vice-versa. Hold the rod at waist height absolutely parallel to the water surface, at no time during the casting action should the rod be raised above waist level.

The back-cast and forward-cast are made in exactly the same manner as our basic casting, but with the rod moving in a horizontal plane instead of a vertical plane.

The side-cast is not difficult to perform, and cuts under the wind to give a very reasonable forward-cast.

A word of warning. You will recall that we discussed the loss of acceleration if the rod was leant over out of the vertical plane during basic casting. Exactly the same applies to the side-cast — if the rod is allowed to move up or down out of the horizontal plane a severe loss of acceleration will be the result.

Note
The side-cast will also be found very useful in a general fishing situation. It is the ideal cast to use when a fly needs to be placed under overhanging foliage. It is also very useful to cast a fly under a low bridge or other obstructions.

Side Winds
A strong side wind can really be troublesome, and also dangerous when blowing directly onto your casting arm. No-one wants a flyline whipping across their face, and a hook travelling at about 50mph is a dangerous object indeed.

Under these circumstances we must be prepared to lose some line acceleration and lean the rod out to the side (into the wind) during the back-cast. During the pause for the back-cast to straighten out, the rod is brought back to the upright position. The forward-cast is then made in the vertical plane.

The effect is to pass the line well to the side of the angler as it travels into the back-cast. The forward-cast will be directly overhead in the normal way — aided by the side wind.

This technique works very well, even in a very strong wind.

Final Comment
When the wind is blowing hard in our faces, and we are striving for distance, long light leaders need to be abandoned. Windy conditions, resulting in choppy water that is slightly discoloured, do not call for long light leaders that will make casting even more difficult. A reasonably heavy 7½ to 9ft tapered leader is all that is required — the fishing will not suffer as a result.

There is no need to follow the crowd who are running away from the wind to fish empty water — we can improve our casting technique and overcome the wind. Technique is the key!

Chapter 7

Curves, Mends, Direction

Up to now we have concentrated on casting a line smoothly and easily a reasonable distance. We have emphasised the various techniques that will enable an angler to improve his casting to a reasonable standard, together with hints that will help to identify faults.

All our efforts will be wasted if the angler only reads the text and studies the illustrations from the comfort of a favourite armchair. It is essential that actual casting takes place, and that this practice casting, (perhaps in the local park over grass) is very carefully analysed and faults corrected. None of this help will be of much use if the practice is left until the next fishing trip. Only some of the information will be remembered, and the need to concentrate on actual fishing will take over. It is hoped that by practice nearer to home the casting will be improved before the next fishing trip is made.

Of course, we must proceed beyond being able to cast a good length of line, we must be able to present a fly that will be taken by a fish. From this point on our practice must take place over water. We will need the inter-action of water surface on the line to aid our technique.

Curves
The river angler will know only too well that a dragging dry fly is rarely taken, and drag on a wet fly or nymph is often just as disastrous. To a lesser extent this also holds true for the angler on stillwater.

Drag may be described as when the fly is moved at an unnatural rate through, or on, the water. The cause may be the pressure of the current on a floating line, or the wind action on a floating line cast on stillwater. In both cases the result at the fly is the same — it moves at a different pace than the current or wind would move a natural insect. An artificial fly moving in this fashion is rarely taken by a wary trout.

There are many ways to overcome this problem, casting a wide curve in the line upstream or upwind, making a hook cast, or pulling back on a forward-cast to cause a slack line, are but a few. The problem is that a high degree of skill is required if such casts are to be effortlessly made. The cast used in the USA, aptly named the 'Lazy S', is the easy way out of the problem.

The 'Lazy S' cast consists of the line landing on the water with a series of slack 'S' bends. Properly performed, only the line will carry the 'S' bends, the leader to the fly will remain straight.

The principle is that the current, or wind, will straighten out the curves before the fly is affected. In the meantime the fly behaves in a natural manner.

To cast a 'Lazy S' is simplicity itself. The basic back-cast is made in the usual manner. On the forward-cast, immediately after the hammer-tap forward is made, and as the line is projecting forward, the rod tip is waggled from side to side as it follows the line down to the water surface. The tip waggling is done very quickly as the line unfurls out in front, only very slight waggling is required (just a series of side to side twitches will do the job). The line follows the rod tip and lands on the water in a series of soft 'S' bends. Very easy and very effective! (*See* Fig.9). For accurate casting don't forget to cast a longer line than needed so as to allow for the slack bends.

Mends
The need to 'mend' a line is brought about by the same circumstances as described above, the current or wind being about to create a belly in the line downstream or downwind of the fly. A mend is of little use when fishing the dry fly as the fly itself will be dragged by the mend, but a wet fly or nymph will be basically undisturbed.

It is surprising how few anglers know how to mend a line correctly (perhaps few casting schools teach this technique) and generally speaking the results commonly seen are simply horrific. There seems to be a general impression that the belly in the line can be lifted off the water and swung over to create a belly of line upstream or downwind. Absolutely not! Such a tactic is rarely successful in creating a good mend, and nearly always the fly is moved in the water. Violent tactics carried out by brute force are so rarely effective in the casting process.

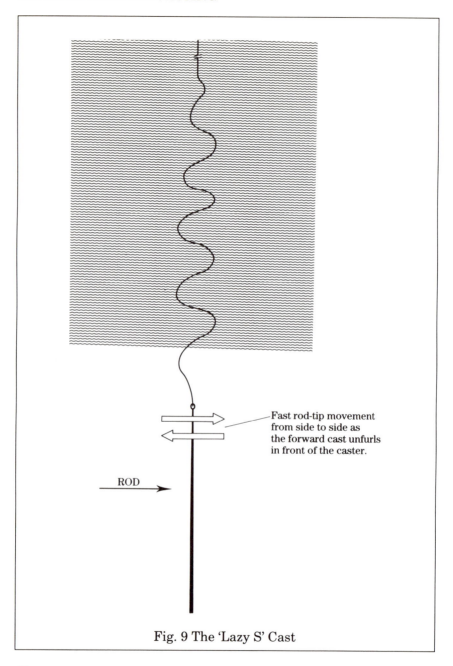

Fast rod-tip movement
from side to side as
the forward cast unfurls
in front of the caster.

ROD

Fig. 9 The 'Lazy S' Cast

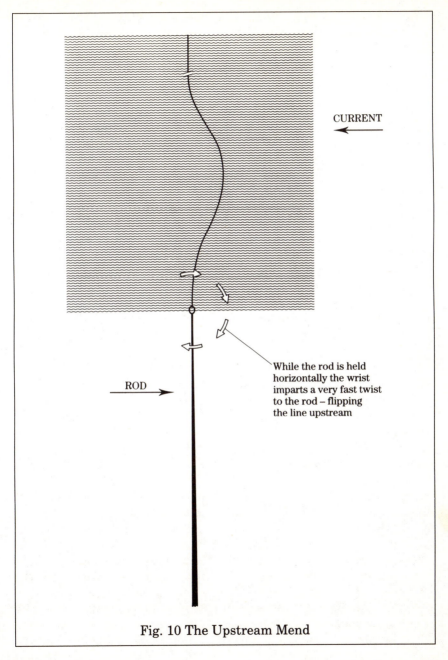

CURRENT

ROD

While the rod is held
horizontally the wrist
imparts a very fast twist
to the rod – flipping
the line upstream

Fig. 10 The Upstream Mend

To be really effective a mend must take place **before** the current or wind has created a belly in the line. It is a matter of anticipation and instinct.

As soon as it appears to the angler that the floating line will be influenced by the current or wind, action needs to be taken. In this manner only a slight mend is necessary, and is easily performed correctly. If the situation calls for more than a slight mend, for instance if the current or wind is so severe that it will quickly absorb the mend already made, then several slight mends should be made in quick succession.

The technique of mending line correctly is simple. The rod is held horizontally at waist height, pointing directly at the fly. A fast sharp twist of the wrist (a half turn) in the direction required, will flip the line over in a slight mend.

If a larger belly in the line is required, repeat the process immediately.

Care should be taken that the rod points directly at the fly; if a succession of mends is made the rod must be re-pointed each time. The rod is never moved from side to side, or up and down, it is just rotated on its axis by a twist of the wrist. Try it for yourself, you will get it right at the first attempt, it couldn't be easier. (*See* Fig.10)

Directions
Very often it is necessary to change the direction of the next cast, in fact, far more often than is generally appreciated. The dry-fly angler will want to pick up at the end of a free float and re-cast again to the same fish, the stillwater angler wishes to cover a sudden rise — one can think of many such instances. Probably the most important is the necessity to 'fan-cast' if stillwater is to be correctly fished. (*See* Fig.11)

Most fly-fishermen fail to realise how often they change the direction of their casting. The dry-fly man goes through the motions of many false casts, changing the direction slowly during each cast. All very fine, but so many false casts are not really necessary, two false casts will invariably dry the fly. The stillwater angler often retrieves practically all the line out, then re-positions himself for the next cast. A lot of work that takes up valuable fishing time.

Perhaps the problem stems from not realising a simple fact — **the line will always follow the path of the rod tip.**

The technique used to change direction simply makes use of the

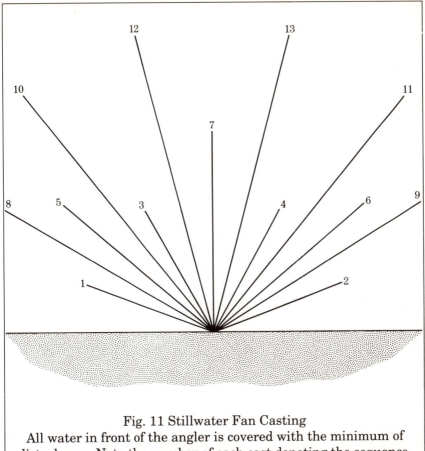

Fig. 11 Stillwater Fan Casting
All water in front of the angler is covered with the minimum of disturbance. Note the number of each cast denoting the sequence. Frequent change of direction is required.

above fact. It is not at all difficult to change direction between the back-cast and the forward-cast up to a 90° angle.

Simply make a standard back-cast, then **during** the brief pause while the line is straightening out — angle your body to face the new direction. The standard forward-cast will send the line in the new direction — **it will follow the rod tip**. It is just as simple as that!

51

Line Kinks and Coils

Casting a straight line, casting 'Lazy S' curves, and mending line, are always very difficult if the fly-line itself is not straight and supple.

P.V.C. lines, and those made with polymer, all have a tendency at times to come off the reel in wavy coils. Even top quality lines have this annoying habit if they have been stored on the reel for a long period. A cold temperature adds to the problem. It is little use thinking that a few casts will sort matters out; after an hour of fishing, the kinks will still be there.

There is only one remedy. Lay the rod down on the grass and draw off 12yd of line from the reel. Starting at the rod tip, stretch each yard of line between the hands. Once along the line should be enough, if not, repeat the process. Now the line will lay straight and give no further problem.

Chapter 8

The Roll Cast

It is probably true to say that of all casting performed, ninety per cent consists of the standard forward and backward cast. However, this should not be so, it is a pointer to the lack of casting proficiency of so many anglers. Although difficult to say how much the roll cast and its variations should be used, it is certain to be quite a large percentage of all casting.

Most anglers know of the roll cast, and many will have tried to master it, but results have probably been very disappointing. From time to time one sees the abysmal efforts being made — no wonder it is so little used.

Without doubt the problems result from a failure to appreciate the basic fundamentals.

The roll cast is comparatively easy to perform, very much easier than basic casting, and anyone can master the technique with less than thirty minutes practice.

Before we deal with the roll cast in detail, let us consider the advantages of using the cast, and when it should, or should not, be used.

Most important, the roll cast enables us to cast a fly without a back-cast as no line is projected behind the angler. Consequently high banks, vegetation, or low foliage to the rear cease to be a problem. Next, it enables us to ensure that wet flies remain wet so that they sink instantly on contact with water. The roll cast will also give us an element of protection from a stiff wind. An additional advantage is the capability of releasing snagged flies, for a roll cast towards a snagged fly will exert a pull in a different direction. Last, but not least, we are able to use a roll cast to pick up a sinking line that is submerged; a well sunken line normally puts a lot of strain on a rod tip, in fact sometimes may even cause a breakage.

There are two other functions of the roll cast, its ability to dispose of surplus loose line in front of the angler, and the advantage of a clean pick-up before a standard back-cast, but more on these points later.

Now for the disadvantages. The roll cast is of very little use to the dry-fly fisherman, for during the cast the line is drawn over the water surface which effectively drowns a dry fly. The angler using a weight forward line, or a shooting head, will also have problems unless **less** than 30ft of line is being used.

Perhaps the best way to bring out the fundamentals of the roll cast is to describe the cast from start to finish. The reader should take it step by step, referring to the illustrations at the end of each stage. Practice can take place at a later time.

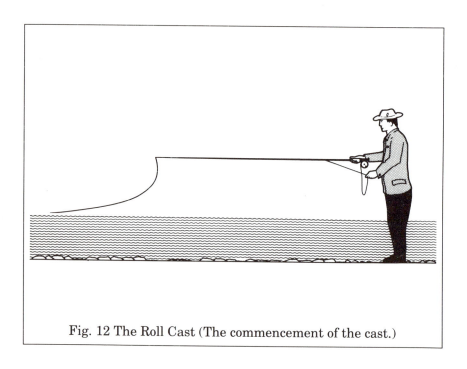

Fig. 12 The Roll Cast (The commencement of the cast.)

Stage (1)

The cast is **always** performed over water, the tension between line and water surface is necessary to load the spring in the rod. Commence the cast with the rod low pointing at the fly. (*See* Fig.12)

Fig. 13 The Roll Cast
(Drawing back the line ready for the pause.)
Note: The rod is laid over out of the vertical plane.

Rear view

Stage (2)

The rod tip is slowly raised to draw the line towards the angler, bringing the fly across, or to, the surface. As the rod tip is raised it is leant out to the side away from the angler (out of the vertical plane), the lean to the side will draw line well away from the angler. The rod continues to rise to the perpendicular, then beyond, to an angle behind the caster. The movement is **slow**, the elbow is still to the side, the rod hand does not pass behind the head. (*See* Fig.13)

55

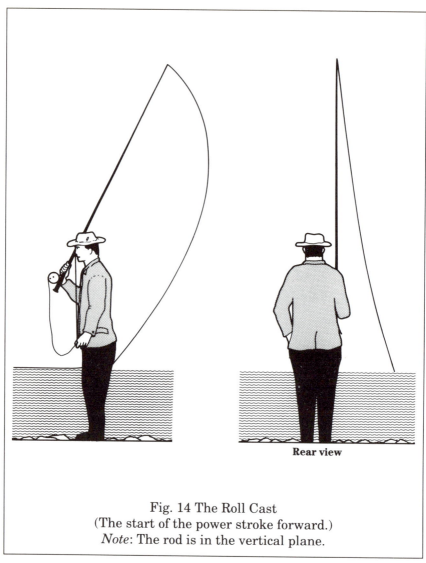

Fig. 14 The Roll Cast
(The start of the power stroke forward.)
Note: The rod is in the vertical plane.

Stage (3)

Once the backward movement is complete, and the line is hanging down from the rod tip, **pause** for the line and rod to settle in position. This pause is essential to enable the full spring of the rod to come into play during the next stage. (*See* Fig.14)

Fig. 15 The Roll Cast
(The end of the forward power stroke.)
Note: The rod is still in the vertical plane. The power stroke
is short. The line rolls out above the water.

Stage (4)

After the pause, move the rod back to the vertical plane and up to the
perpendicular, then make a **short**, hammer-like forward-cast straight
out to the front.

Note: This stage is all one movement, a continuous smooth action.

The tension between line and water will activate the spring in the
rod, the line will roll forward in an unfurling loop **above** the water.
At the end of the cast the rod tip follows the line down to the water in
the usual way. (*See* Fig.15)

A lot of description, but very necessary to bring out the fundamental points of a cast that is basically quite simple.

The following check-list of common mistakes may help when practice commences.

Roll Cast — Common Mistakes
1 Rod is **not** leant to the side during Stage (2)
2 Line is not drawn back **slowly** during Stage (2)
3 No **pause** is made at stage (3)
4 Rod is **not** raised to vertical plane for Stage (4)
5 Forward power stroke is **too hard** in Stage (4)
6 Forward power stroke is **not short enough** in Stage (4)

Useful Variations
It has already been mentioned that the roll cast can be used to dispose of surplus line in front of the angler. It often happens when drawing off line prior to casting, or after a fly has been changed, or a fish caught and netted, that excessive line is hanging from the rod tip. Going through the motions of a roll cast will send the surplus line out across the water ready to be picked up and projected into a back-cast.

Another useful variation of the roll cast is to use it in combination with a basic back-cast. If a sinking line is in use, and is deeply submerged at the end of a retrieve, a roll cast will bring it to the surface without undue strain on the rod tip. The roll cast is made in the normal manner — but, **immediately after** the forward power stroke a standard back-cast is made.

It may well seem very strange, and quite unnerving, to commence a standard back-cast whilst a line is still rolling in a loop to the front. Don't worry! The loop will straighten out and the line be projected to the rear without difficulty.

A back-cast that is made in the above fashion has a very high line acceleration due to the spring in the rod being heavily loaded by the unfurling loop of line. The result is the ability to cast a long forward-cast — another way to obtain distance by technique!

Most rods will perform a reasonable roll cast, but difficulty may be experienced with some of the older split-cane rods. Most modern carbon rods are either tip-action or full flex, and both will perform a roll cast with ease. An old split-cane rod with a so-called wet fly action, a full butt-action rod, will never perform a roll cast well. However, today there are few of these rods in use.

Mastering the roll cast brings many benefits to the fly-fisher, it is essential that the cast becomes part of the casting repertoire if future progress is to be made.

Chapter 9

Variations

An experienced caster, very well used to handling line, employs all sorts of variations to present his fly to the right place. Sometimes these variations are combinations of standard techniques, a roll cast may be combined with multiple mends, or a roll cast combined with a back-cast then a 'Lazy S' forward-cast, etc., etc.

When fishing small streams a very experienced angler will sometimes fish from one stream feature to another with a series of flicks and mends, almost without casting at all. Such an activity is a joy to watch — it is supreme handling of a fly-line.

However such activities come with wide experience and are mainly self-taught, we cannot hope to cover such a high degree of line handling in these pages. Provided an angler reaches a high level of competence in basic casting, plus actual fishing experience, the rest will surely follow.

The variations we are going to discuss here are standard casts, only classified as variations because of the different techniques required.

We have already dealt with the roll cast, so useful to overcome obstructions to a standard back-cast, but for many reasons a roll cast is not always desirable. Sometimes we need to cast from the most difficult places — that's often where the fish are — and a different approach is necessary.

A small stillwater comes to mind that had open banks except for a small section that was heavily wooded. A narrow path ran along the bank, but the trees closely bordered the path, a back-cast from such a situation was impossible. Needless to say, the best fish were often to be found in that section. There were several small gaps in the foliage, but extreme accuracy was necessary to find the gaps.

It was amusing to see an angler who had turned his back to the water and was aiming his forward-cast between a gap in the trees, he was using his back-cast to deliver the fly to the water! Ingenious as this may be, the technique does not lend itself to good fly presentation, and certainly accuracy is out of the question.

The only real answer to such a problem lies in the steeple cast.

The Steeple Cast

It must be said at the outset that a true steeple cast is sixty per cent theory, twenty per cent technique and twenty per cent pure luck. In its true form it is a most difficult cast to perform well, but provided only a short cast (**less** than 30ft of line past the rod tip) is attempted, the result can be quite good.

The theory is to project the back-cast straight up in the air, straight above the caster's head, then, after the appropriate pause, to make a forward-cast in the normal manner. (*See* Fig.18)

All well and good, but how does one project such a high back-cast when lifting a length of line off the water? The very act of raising the rod to lift off the line sends the back-cast straight back. So much for pure theory! As mentioned above, a reasonable result can be obtained with a very short length of line, but a normal length cast will not respond at all.

However, a combination cast will do the trick.

Start with the line extended over the water. Make a standard roll cast, but on the forward power stroke aim the cast much higher, well above eye level. As the line rolls out to the front (well above the water), immediately project the line into the steeple back-cast. Remember, **the line always follows the rod tip**, so make sure that the rod stops short of the perpendicular on the back-cast. (*See* Figs.16, 17 & 18)

Another situation where a modified steeple cast can be useful is when fishing from a very steep bank; such situations are often encountered when reservoir fishing. Usually there are no actual obstructions to the rear, but the steepness of the bank causes constant hang-ups on the back-cast. The situation does not call for a true steeple cast, but if the motions of a standard steeple cast are carried out the annoying hang-ups will be avoided. In this instance the longer length of line being cast is no handicap; it will prevent a true steeple cast, but an extremely high back-cast will be the result.

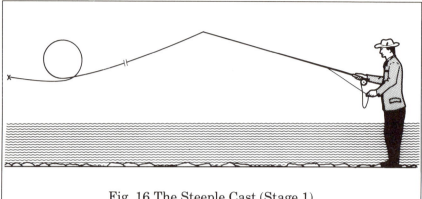

Fig. 16 The Steeple Cast (Stage 1)
The roll cast has been made high over the water,
ready for the back-cast.

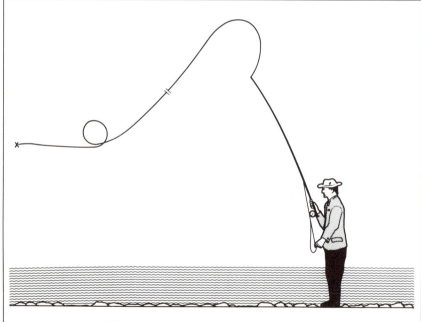

Fig. 17 The Steeple Cast (Stage 2)
The power stroke into the back-cast has commenced.
Note: The line is still unrolling to the front.

Fig. 18 The Steeple Cast (Stage 3)
The back-cast has been completed.
The forward-cast can now be made in the normal way.
Note: The rod is short of the vertical so as to drive the line upwards.

The Bow and Arrow Cast

This cast used to be a favourite of long ago, these days it is very seldom used. Perhaps the very long rods used in bygone days lent themselves to this cast; the shorter rods of today are not really built for it. Nevertheless, it can be very useful at times, but today few anglers are familiar with it.

The main use of the bow and arrow cast is to fish those nearby spots where any form of cast is impossible. We all know of such situations; standing on a ledge under a bridge, balanced on one foot down a steep bank among dense foliage etc. The cast (it really isn't a cast at all) can only be made with about 7ft of line beyond the rod tip. However, if we add together the rod length, say 9ft, plus leader 9ft, plus arm length 3ft, we are able to reach fish up to about 28ft away.

The technique is to lower the rod to the horizontal, draw off about 7ft of line and, using the left line-holding hand, take a very firm grip of the line between the fingers. The point to hold is where the line joins the leader. Let the leader and fly hang loosely down. Trap the line from the reel firmly under the rod-holding hand.

Now, with the rod still horizontal, put a very good bend in the rod by pulling the rod horizontally to the right. Aim the rod tip to where you want the fly to alight, hold the rod firmly in that position and release your left hand hold on the line. The bend in the rod will straighten and shoot the fly to where it is required. Remember, **the line follows the rod tip**. (*See* Fig.19)

'Bow and Arrow' is a pretty good description, and it works well in very close quarters.

As you gain proficiency don't be afraid to combine techniques and different casts, it is the way forward to mastering line control — the hallmark of an experienced caster.

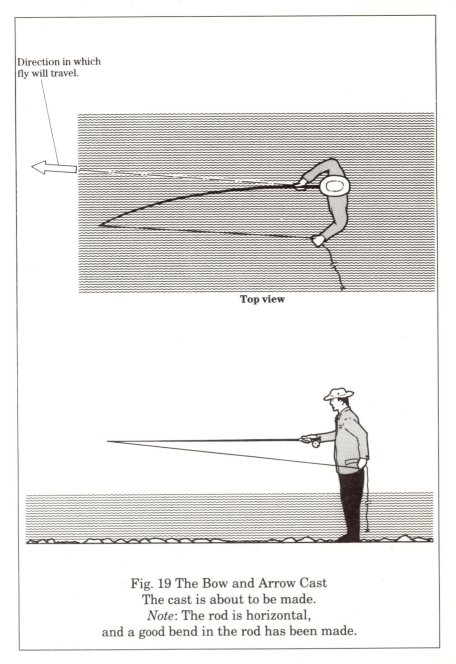

Direction in which
fly will travel.

Top view

Fig. 19 The Bow and Arrow Cast
The cast is about to be made.
Note: The rod is horizontal,
and a good bend in the rod has been made.

Chapter 10

Rolls, Mends and Retrieves

We have discussed the techniques of the roll cast, mending line, and executing slack casts. Now comes the time to put these techniques together into a fishing situation.

The wet fly fishing method that has been dubbed 'sweeping a pool', has been fully described in print elsewhere, and may now be familiar to some readers. The method requires a unique combination of casting techniques that up to this point may not have been in the repertoire of the average angler, but now the method should be easy to use.

As a matter of general interest, the following account tells how 'sweeping the pool' originated.

Some years ago we were fishing the Beaverkill in the Catskill region of New York State, USA. The Beaverkill is probably the most famous trout stream in the eastern US, being the home water of Theodore Gordon, the father of US dry fly fishing. The river is steeped in fly-fishing history, and is also the water of the American Fly-Fisher's Club.

Although a splendid trout water, it is very heavily fished due to the dense population of New York State, New York City being within driving distance. The fish are certainly there, but are notoriously difficult to catch, a considerable degree of skill is needed to have a really good day.

Our own results on that particular day had been poor, and by lunchtime we had nothing to show for our efforts. We decided to relax and have lunch sitting on the bank of a well known junction pool.

Idly we watched a couple of small boys fishing the pool in front of us. Neither of the boys was actually casting, they were moving slowly down the pool mending their lines to the right and left, allowing their flies to play in the current in wide arcs.

The whole point of this story is that they were catching fish! A lot of fish!

Any technique that will take a number of fish from such a difficult water is well worth a closer scrutiny and refinement. So, let us consider this 'sweeping' technique in detail.

To 'sweep a pool' with wet flies we make a start at the head of a suitable long pool. It is a wading technique from the stream centre, so the pool has to be reasonably shallow. (*See* Figs. 20, 21, 22)

First use a roll cast to extend about 10yd of line, then allow the current to straighten out the line downstream. Now make another roll cast towards the left bank, the current will take over and 'sweep' the flies to the stream centre. As the flies swing to the central position they will rise in the current and play close to the water surface. Allow a few moments, then retrieve the flies with a jerky retrieve for a few feet. Now mend the line well to the right — several mends if necessary. The flies will now 'sweep' to the right as the line straightens in the current. Once the line is straight the current will, once again, swing the flies to the stream centre in a rising arc. The process is now repeated — a pause followed by a short retrieve — then a series of mends to the left to repeat the first sequence. At the end of each sequence move down the stream a couple of paces, then repeat the process again from left to right.

Sounds complicated? Have a look at Figs. 20, 21 and 22, then read the text again, it will soon become quite clear.

The reason this is such a successful way to fish the wet fly should now be very apparent. The wet fly is hardly ever out of the water — the whole pool is covered from left to right throughout the pool length — there are periods of deep 'free drift' — periods of retrieve — raising arcs to the surface — deep swinging arcs. Almost all wet fly techniques amalgamated at one time.

No wonder those small boys of the Catskills were catching fish!

The 'sweeping' technique works even better if a weighted fly is used, but if using a team of flies it is only necessary to weight the point fly. Split shot should never be used, no matter how small the shot it will affect the roll cast, and the mends will not create a smooth 'sweep'.

Fig. 20 'Sweeping a Pool' (Stage 1)
Roll cast to 'A' then allow the current to swing the flies in a rising arc to 'B'. Retrieve flies by a jerky retrieve to 'C'.

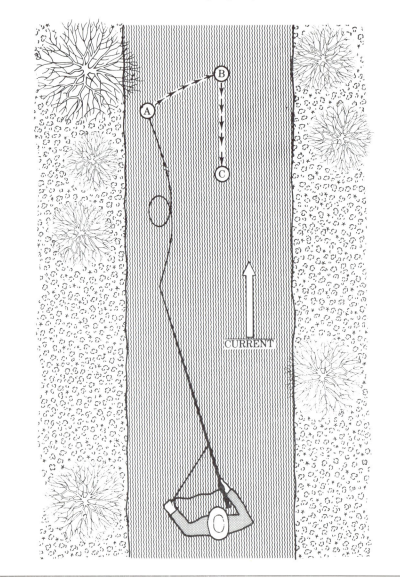

Fig. 21 'Sweeping a Pool' (Stage 2)

From 'C' make a series of mends to the right. Allow the current to swing the flies to 'D' as line is paid out. From 'D' the current will swing the flies to 'E' as the line straightens. Retrieve flies to 'F' by means of a jerky retrieve.

Note: Now step forward a few paces and repeat stages (1) and (2).

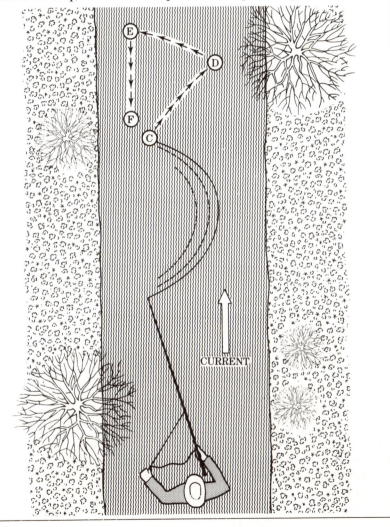

CURRENT

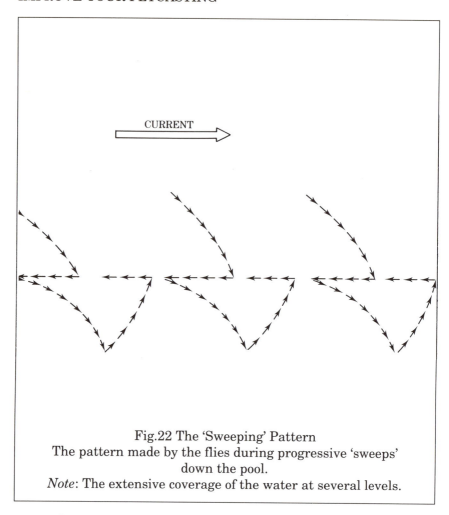

Fig.22 The 'Sweeping' Pattern
The pattern made by the flies during progressive 'sweeps'
down the pool.
Note: The extensive coverage of the water at several levels.

As the years have gone by 'sweeping the pool' has produced many fine fish from a variety of waters. A very fine wild brown (he must have been king of the river), was taken whilst 'sweeping' a remote Welsh mountain pool. A long way from the Catskills!

Quite apart from being a successful technique, 'sweeping' allows us to practice to perfection all we have learned about rolls, mends and retrieves. It also shows us how necessary it is to learn those skills if we are to take advantage of all fishing methods and situations.

Chapter 11

Taking Aim

The title of this chapter is somewhat misleading, we are not talking about aiming at a particular point or fish, our subject is the height of the forward-cast.

When we make a forward-cast we 'aim' the line out to the front, it is important to know at what level we need to aim the cast. Basically speaking we can aim high (above eye level), at eye level, or we can aim downwards towards the water. There are good reasons for all these levels, but there are also drawbacks that must be taken into consideration. It would be very wrong to aim all our casts at the same level, regardless of the fishing situation.

The Downward Cast

A deliberate downward cast is not used that often — nor should it be — as it is basically poor casting technique. A downward cast will usually result in the line landing on the water before the leader and fly, and the unfurling line causes considerable disturbance on the water surface. If enough skill is used to keep the line off the water until the fly has alighted, then the fly presentation will be a little rough.

However, there are times when such a presentation is desirable. Very often anglers using terrestrial lures, such as grasshoppers, beetles and caterpillars, require the offering to arrive on the water with a distinct plop. Trout are very much attracted to terrestrials that land on the water in this manner.

It is also a fact that a normal forward-cast into the wind will invariably result in the leader failing to straighten out. The fly just blows back in a curve. A forward-cast aimed low will cut under the wind and allow the leader to straighten out before landing on the water.

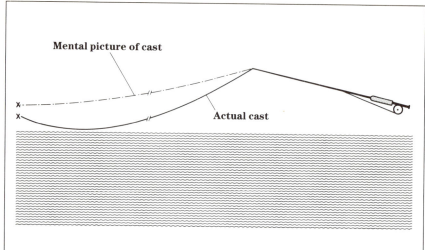

Fig. 23 Aiming a Downward Cast
A poorly performed downward cast.
The rod tip has preceded the fly down to the water.
Note: The line is unfurling on the water before the fly alights.

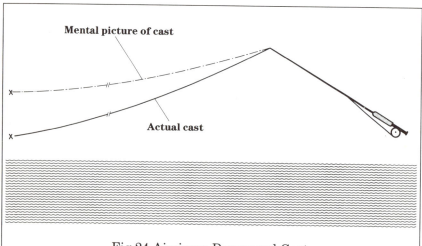

Fig 24 Aiming a Downward Cast
A correctly aimed downward forward-cast. The rod tip has
followed the line down, the fly will reach the water before the line.

All-in-all, aiming a cast downwards is not a good idea unless you have a specific reason for doing so. If the majority of your forward-casts are inclined to be low, then look to your technique to put the matter right. Remember, only a 'hammer-tap' forward is necessary, and the rod tip should **follow** the line down to the water — not precede it. (*See* Figs. 23, 24)

The Upward Cast

An upward aimed forward-cast, unlike a downward cast, is a very useful cast to cultivate.

It must be realised that, no matter how well a forward-cast is executed, the line begins to fall as soon as the cast is made. It may well appear to travel out smoothly and retain its level, but like all other objects it is subject to gravity. A very long cast needs to be aimed a little high to enable the line to completely unfurl before the target area is reached.

A highly aimed forward-cast is also necessary when making a 'Lazy S' cast, the higher line will give time to form the 'S' bends before the line descends to the water surface.

The above also applies to the so-called 'Reach Cast', but we have not yet dealt with this cast — more on that later.

Another reason for aiming a high forward-cast is when casting with your back to the wind. Under such circumstances an extremely long cast can be made if the forward-cast is aimed high. The wind will carry the line well, and will help it unfurl beautifully before it reaches the target area.

However, there are distinct problems with a high forward-cast that should also be appreciated.

Under normal conditions too high a cast will result in the line completely unfurling before it reaches the water surface. The often seen 'bird's nest' of leader round the fly is evidence of such a cast, the leader having fallen from a height with little or no forward momentum. All forward energy being expended whilst the leader was much too high above the water surface.

The above problem does not arise with a 'Lazy S' or 'Reach Cast', as all slack in the line is removed during the forward-cast and the forward momentum at the fly is maintained.

Another problem with a very high forward-cast arises when casting into a wind. The wind will have more opportunity of catching the line, the result is nearly always a failure to straighten out the line.

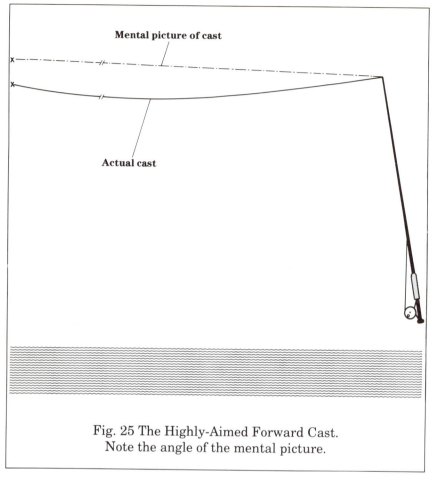

Fig. 25 The Highly-Aimed Forward Cast.
Note the angle of the mental picture.

Sometimes in a high wind the line may even blow back towards the angler. (*See* Fig.25)

Eye Level Casts
Most forward-casts are aimed at eye level — but don't forget, the mental picture is forward and **upward** for this to be achieved. The eye level cast should be accepted as the 'norm', only special circumstances require a variation to be made. However, it is necessary for good casting that the variations be fully understood and called into play as required.

The Reach-cast
The reader may know how to perform the reach-cast, or at least know of it. Anglers who have attended a casting school, or had professional instruction, can probably perform the cast reasonably well.

The problem is that the cast is almost impossible to describe in print. Illustrations are of very little help as the cast is made through two dimensions and is most difficult to portray clearly.

The reach-cast is used to overcome drag when fishing the dry fly. A very basic description could be that it is a variation performed during a forward-cast. As the forward-cast unfurls in front of the angler the rod tip is moved to the left, or right, so as to lay the line on the water upstream of the fly.

The problem with such a description is that it does not, and cannot, explain how the action of the forward stroke is maintained whilst the rod is moved out of the vertical plane. Just laying over the rod tip will not achieve the cast — in fact it will ruin it.

Only the instructor, working directly with a pupil, can clearly teach such a cast. However, all is not lost. The object of a reach-cast is to overcome drag, it allows some line that can be acted upon by the current before the fly is affected. The 'Lazy S' cast (previously fully described and illustrated) will do exactly the same job.

If you can avail yourself of personal professional instruction, then the reach-cast is well worth learning. In the meantime the 'Lazy S' cast will serve very well to overcome most fly dragging situations.

Chapter 12

Misconceptions

On looking over all that has been written in the preceding pages, it seems that little mention has been made of several popular misconceptions. Emphasis has been laid on the correct approach to casting, and this must be right, but it is also necessary to put to rest (permanently) a number of common misconceptions that will impair progress.

A number of experienced casters are basically satisfied — or almost satisfied — with the distance they obtain, some are even proud of their efforts. All well and good, if the cast is made with finesse, but is the 'finesse of a cast' truly appreciated?

Distance alone is just not good enough. It is of little use obtaining extreme distance if the cast slashes across the water like the cut of a knife. We have all seen these casts, the impact of the line on the water surface can be seen for a considerable distance. Sometimes, when fishing a stillwater, the length of another angler's cast can be seen a couple of hundred yards away.

Such casting cannot be admired. Not only are all the fish disturbed in the area of the faulty cast, but frightened fish disturb others as they dash for safety. Our own fishing is probably adversely affected.

The pity of the situation is that the offending angler is so seldom aware of the problems he creates, often he is so pleased with the distance that he is oblivious to the disturbance.

The problem is quite simple to remedy. The fault lies in the forward-cast — the rod is **preceding** the line to the water surface, instead of **following** the line down. Remember, **the line follows the rod tip**; if you bring the rod tip down towards the water with a vicious forward stroke, the line will react in exactly the same manner.

Let us now look at another common misconception.

Many casters, having difficulty in performing their back-cast, are advised to look back when they cast so that the line remains in view. The theory seems to be that you will be able to control the line because you can see it. Not so! Once the rod (our spring), has done its work correctly and projected the line, the course of the back-cast is committed. The back-cast is not capable of being varied whilst in flight — not unless the motions of the back-cast have been incorrectly made in the first place.

Even worse, the very act of turning the body, and head, to view the cast creates a major problem. The correct casting stance is destroyed, the rod movement is probably out of the vertical plane, and line acceleration is reduced to a minimum. In fact, the line will just flow back and forth in a slow wide arc.

If the back-cast is giving difficulty it is necessary to go back to basics. Shorten the cast, pay attention to all the fundamentals, then, when things are going well resume normal distance. Looking back will do nothing for you whatsoever.

The practice of using multiple flies on the leader, connected by droppers, is an old fishing technique of many year's standing. Without doubt it works, but how is the casting affected? Have no doubt the effects are considerable. The multi-fly technique originated when the average rod length seen on rivers was anything up to 18ft long. Lines were not cast as they are today, the team of flies was almost dangled in the water below the rod tip, just a flick of the long rod was sufficient to move the flies from place to place. On lakes and lochs most fishing took place from boats that drifted in the wind, no distance casting was necessary. This 'loch style' fishing is still very popular on the reservoirs today.

When we apply the modern techniques of distance casting, using modern equipment, multi-flies on our leaders cause difficulties. Many anglers, seemingly unaware of the problems, just carry on as usual as if a standard one fly cast was being made. All sorts of tangles result, the dropper flies wrap round the leader, flies even hook up in the line/leader connection.

A multi-fly cast needs to be made with the back-cast and forward-cast in a slower wider loop (termed a 'broad entry'). However, distance is obtained from line acceleration, and 'broad entry' casts cannot create line acceleration. So, the idea that you can use a multi-fly set-up, **and** obtain distance by double-haul casting, is just not so.

At this point we should mention 'wind knots', for they are so often associated with multi-fly casts. 'Wind knots' are **not** caused by wind, they are caused by a poor casting technique that does not form a uniform loop in the line. The result is that the leader doubles over itself and knots are formed. Poor rod acceleration into the back-cast causes a wavy line, if followed by an insufficient pause for the line to straighten out — presto, you have a wind knot! A hard forward-cast instead of a light 'hammer-tap' and you produce a bounce-back at the end of the cast — another wind knot! Blaming the wind is a waste of time, only you are responsible for those horrid little knots. (*See* Fig. 26)

Another false theory that badly affects casting is that fine tippets are always good fishing practice. Not necessarily so. Of course we must insist on the finest tippet it is possible to use, but it must be **consistent with the fly size and weight**. If you insist on using size 8 or size 10 flies, or your flies are weighted to sink, then you cannot use ultra fine nylon for tippets. The reverse is also true; small nymphs or dry flies in sizes 16 to 20 cannot be properly presented on heavy tippets. We are not governed by the size of fish we hope to catch, we are governed by the fly size and fly weight. If you ignore the above fact the result will be a very poor presentation, plus excessive wind knots, or perhaps even the loss of the fly during the casting process. Your leader and tippet must be balanced to the fly in the same manner as your line is balanced to the rod.

There are so many misconceptions, and we can only deal with a few in these pages. The misconceptions that apply to casting must be our main concern.

Many anglers are constantly concerned about the height of their back-cast. Somehow, no matter how high they aim the cast, there is always the subconscious feeling that it is dropping low. Often the surmise is proved correct, the cast hits the water or ground behind the caster.

More often than not the line weight is considered suspect, and that is the misconception. True, an incorrect line weight will cause such problems, but in nearly all cases the caster is at fault. A line weight has to be considerably in error before it can cause consistently low back-casts.

To truly analyse the situation it is necessary to carefully watch the forward-cast, for this will faithfully reflect the quality of the back-cast. If the forward-cast is wavy with a wide loop (known as a 'broad entry'), then the quality of the back-cast leaves a lot to be desired. The caster needs to make adjustments to his motions.

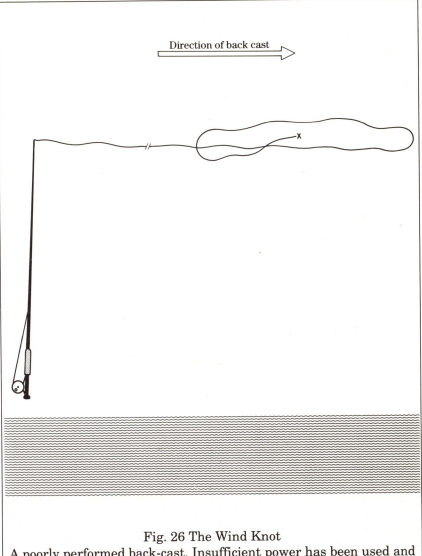

Fig. 26 The Wind Knot
A poorly performed back-cast. Insufficient power has been used and
the rod tip carried too far back beyond the vertical.
Note: The result is the inability of the line to straighten out
and exert force on the rod tip. Note also that a 'wind knot'
has started to develop.

IMPROVE YOUR FLYCASTING

The most common mistake is allowing the rod tip to travel too far back, or, to put it another way, failing to stop the power stroke at the perpendicular. Most casters make this error, and most casters honestly believe they don't.

The remedy lies with the mental picture we have already discussed (remember?), we must have a mental picture of the line being projected **upwards**. Never **backwards**.

A contributing mistake is too short a pause to allow the line to straighten out. Of course there will be the feeling that a longer pause will allow the cast to fall, but it won't happen if the cast has been correctly made.

The problem is that a bad back-cast results in a poor forward-cast — and the poor forward-cast makes the next back-cast even worse.

Perseverance, practice, and self criticism will solve most problems.

Chapter 13

Style

Without doubt a major hindrance to teaching good basic casting is the various styles of casting seen at any waterside. Many anglers, trying hard to improve their own casting, are confronted by others who cast in a totally different manner, but are achieving much better results.

It is only too easy to become disheartened when someone else, who appears to be doing everything wrong, gets good results. Even worse, some instructors have a style entirely their own and are almost incapable of demonstrating what they are insisting upon.

Style is a very individual thing that develops with experience. It is impossible to learn casting by attempting to copy another angler's style that has taken years to develop.

If we accept that style develops with experience, and if a particular style is getting good results, we must also accept that the style is based on good sound theory.

Let us try and explain this apparent paradox. A famous golfer, a winner of many tournaments, may well have a swing that is entirely his own. It would be an absolute disaster for anyone learning the game to try and copy his style. The famous man's swing has developed after many years' experience. It has very slowly evolved to exactly suit his build, muscle structure, and his built-in sense of timing. His swing is entirely his own personal thing.

However, we must not delude ourselves into thinking that our imaginary golf 'pro' started out that way — that would be impossible. Such a high degree of skill could never have been attained without a solid basic foundation, the very individual style developed later.

The aim of this little book has been to build that solid basic foundation.

As the years go by we all develop a style of our own. We all vary in build, muscle power, size, etc., and consequently various slight changes creep into our casting to compensate for these things. These changes take place without us even realising they are happening. Changes, very subtle ones, also take place as we get older — style evolves naturally over a long period of time.

The most important thing is for the foundation to be correctly and soundly laid. All principles and fundamentals must be fully understood, they must become automatic and instinctive. All great casters, regardless of individual style, are fully aware of the basic principles.

Under no circumstances try and improve your casting by copying the particular style of someone else, regardless of how successful that person is. Build your own solid foundation and let your own style slowly develop over a period of time.

One day someone will watch your particular style, will see how effective it is, and be tempted to try and copy it. Little will they realise that hidden beneath your style is a solid knowledge of basic casting skills.

So far we have discussed casting as generally performed in Great Britain, and have used tackle that is widely accepted as standard this side of the Atlantic. Although the principles and fundamentals will always remain constant, styles around the world vary to suit fishing conditions, and the particular variety of gamefish angled for.

For instance, in North America freshwater bass fishing has developed into a separate form of fly-fishing — the tackle and casting style being peculiar to that species. In a like manner, 'saltwater fly rodding', as our American friends so aptly call it, has developed into a completely separate sport. Tackle and casting style bear no resemblance to our gamefishing in the UK.

We must not confuse these totally different sports. True, they have the same base, but so do tennis, squash and badminton (a strung racquet). We would hardly try and improve our tennis by watching a game of squash!

In the USA, there is, or was at one time, an exclusive club called the '20/20 club'. Membership consisted of anglers who had landed 20lb fish on a size 20 fly!!! This fad led to a virtual cult in tackle. Rods of 5ft length, lines of Nos. 2 and 3 weight, leaders and tippets to suit the small flies.

It was mentioned earlier that rods shorter than 7ft required a totally different casting technique, consequently the casting style of the short rod exponents does nothing to help us.

However, it must be admitted that the late Lee Wulff of the USA was a joy to watch when he cast with a 5ft rod. He was an artist with a style entirely his own, but his casting school on the Beaverkill, nevertheless, specialises in the teaching of good, basic fundamentals.

As a final word, admire different styles by all means, but make no attempt to copy them. Develop your own style over a period of time. Let your own style naturally evolve from a solid foundation that was achieved by perseverance and practice.

Enjoy your casting!